Cuisinart Toaster Oven Air Fryer Cookbook 1000

Easy Tasty Recipes Guide to air fry, convection bake, convection broil, bake, broil, Warm and toast by Your Cuisinart convection Toaster Oven Air Fryer

By Jonathan Miller

Table of Contents

Description

A complete cookbook consisting of the easiest and tastiest recipes that you can attempt making with the Cuisinart TOA-60 Convection Toaster Oven Airfryer today!

The cookbook consists of fun and important tips and tricks as a bonus. In this cookbook, you will be offered a wide range of amazing and delicious recipes that you can cook in your prized toaster oven Air Fryer.

The cookbook consists of:
- What the Cuisinart TOA-60 Convection Toaster Oven Airfryer is
- How the Gadget Works
- Tips and Tricks for Usage and Operation
- Basic Matters That Need Attention
- Simply Ways to Clean and Maintain the Toaster Oven Airfryer
- 80 Fun and Delicious Recipes to Try Out!

Recipes are divided into various chapters, including:
- Brunches
- Beef, Pork, & Lamb
- Fish & Seafood
- Chicken & Poultry
- Vegan & Vegetarian
- Baking Recipes
- Roasting Recipes
- Desserts and Snacks

Waste no time in taking a dive into this detailed and versatile cookbook full of delicious recipes waiting for you to try out.

Introduction

Technology has brought forth a lot of amazing and unique gadgets that are meant to make everyday lives of busy people easier and more convenient to deal with. One such amazing gadget that has taken the home and kitchen appliance sector by storm is a convection toaster oven airfryer.

Sustainable and technologically advanced toaster oven air fryers are now one of the most sought after kitchen appliances, mainly due to how easy such a gadget is to use and the various functions that it offers to users.

There are plenty of amazing manufacturers boasting convection toaster oven air fryers. However, one brand that typically stands out is none other than Cuisinart.

Complete with incredible features and ideal specifications that one demands in a typical kitchen appliance, Cuisinart makes sure to include everything in its best TOA-60 Convection Toaster Oven Airfryer.

This highly efficient and versatile Cuisinart TOA-60 Convection Toaster Oven Airfryer is designed in a way to reduce all your cooking worries to a bare minimum. The gadget is meant to turn even the most unhealthy, oily recipes into fun, delicious and nutritious meals!

How is that possible, you ask? Sit tight as this cookbook will guide you through all the stuff you need to know (including the good, the bad and the ugly) about the product in general, while also covering some amazing recipes later in the cookbook that you can try out in the Cuisinart TOA-60 Convection Toaster Oven Airfryer.

Cuisinart TOA-60 Convection Toaster Oven Airfryer

Right off the bat, the Cuisinart TOA-60 Convection Toaster Oven Airfryer is a force to be reckoned with. The gadget does everything that you could possibly imagine a toaster oven do while also incorporating the features of an airfryer that not only ensures quality food but also a healthy and nutritious meal consumption.

The innovative design of the product makes sure that it fits perfectly on any kitchen countertop. Compared to traditional toaster ovens, the size and build of this Cuisinart TOA-60 Convection Toaster Oven Airfryer is compact and lightweight.

You can literally place it on any countertop without having to worry about moving the product when you want to cook something up.

On top of that, the Cuisinart TOA-60 Convection Toaster Oven Airfryer comes equipped with sturdy rubber feet that hold up the gadget in place so that it does not budge or move around during operation.

How the Gadget Works

Such an amazing gadget is bound to come with a range of incredible features that distinguish it from its competitors. The Cuisinart TOA-60 Convection Toaster Oven Airfryer is one of the most versatile kitchen appliances on the market at the moment.

The features and specifications of it are easy to understand and make use of, which in turn makes the product highly suitable for usage by beginners.

The array of functions on Cuisinart TOA-60 Convection Toaster Oven Airfryer is meant to allow users to cook and create whatever they set their minds to. Complete with its simple and minimalistic design and external interface, there is nothing you can't do with such an equipment in your kitchen!

In order to maintain its sturdy and durable external appearance, the Cuisinart TOA-60 Convection Toaster Oven Airfryer is constructed with high quality stainless steel. Inside, the product features a non-stick design in order to ensure that food does not stick while being cooked or baked.

Some of the noteworthy features and functions that the Cuisinart TOA-60 Convection Toaster Oven Airfryer comes with are pointed out below.

1. **1800 Watt-** This convection toaster oven air fryer operates on an electrical output of 1800 Watts only.

2. **Power Light-** Say goodbye to confusions regarding the doneness of your meal inside a toaster oven airfryer! This gadget comes with a simple yet handy power light that accurately shows when the oven is in use and when it is kept idle.

3. **Temperature Dial-** This handy dial is what will allow you to check and tweak the temperature of the oven.

4. **Timer Dial-** On the other hand, you can set up a specific time limit for cooking and baking on the airfryer. Note that this feature works only for the airfryer (meaning the toaster oven does not support this function).

5. **Crumb Tray-** For ease of usage and simple cleaning, the toaster oven air fryer also includes a crumb tray inside the product that you can pull out after cooking or baking.

6. **Oven Rack-** The oven rack is available to be used in two different ways. Firstly, you can either pull it halfway out the oven for air frying and broiling the food. Secondly, you can take it all the way out in order to toast whatever you want.

7. **Drip Tray-** For users' convenience, a drip tray is equipped inside the toaster oven airfryer. This tray will collect liquid dough or excess oil during baking and airfrying.

8. **Light Button-** Cooking at night will be a joy with the light button that comes with this gadget. You can turn the interior oven light on during usage of the gadget.

But don't worry about forgetting to turn the feature off when not using the product, as the equipment makes sure to do so itself when left idle for a while.

9. **Cord Storage-** Bid goodbye to messy cords on the counter top as this convection toaster oven air fryer comes with a cord storage compartment equipped on the back side of the gadget.

10. **Whisper Quiet Operation-** You can expect minimal noise when the toaster oven air fryer is in use. The Whisper Quiet Operation function allows you to use the product even in the dead of the night!

11. **Baking-** You can bake all kinds of cakes and muffins, or whatever your heart desires with this toaster oven airfryer. The gadget has a fan on the

inside which circulates heat in all directions, so that user's consume thoroughly baked goodies afterwards.

12. **Toasting-** As mentioned above, the second position of the oven rack allows toasting buns and other doughy goodies.

13. **Broiling-** You can also broil any kind of meat, including fish in this airfryer. If you want to go for traditional broiling, you are suggested to avoid using the convection broiling feature.

14. **Pizza-** Bake the tastiest and freshest pizza with this amazing convection toaster oven air fryer without having to opt for unhealthy fast food joints every time you get a craving!

You can air fry the following food items with this convection toaster oven air fryer by Cuisinart:

- *Chicken wings-* Cook time for this is only around 10 minutes in total, including preparation and heating

- *Frozen nuggets-* Frozen nuggets will require an airfrying time of 10 minutes only

- *Shrimp-* You can expect healthy, and delicious shrimp being cooked under 15 minutes

- *Hand-cut fries-* Hand cut fries will take around 15 minutes or so to be perfectly fried

- *Steak fries-* Steak fries take only 20 minutes or so to be cooked to perfection in this airfryer

- *Mozzarella sticks-* From popcorn shrimp to mozzarella sticks, you will be required to invest less than 10 minutes of total fry time

- *Tortilla chips-* Tortilla chips will require about 6 minutes to be cooked completely. Remember to toss them over around the 3 minutes mark

- **_Bacon-_**You can air fry bacon within 10 minutes only.

Tips and Tricks for Usage and Operation

Using and operating the Cuisinart TOA-60 Convection Toaster Oven Airfryer is actually not a hard thing to do at all. Firstly, users will be provided with an instruction manual guide anyway, which reduces chances of confusion regarding technical jargon.

Other than that, the product itself is very easy and simple to maneuver around with. For example, you can bake and cook everything starting from pizza to whole chicken and turkey roasts and even bite-sized cookies and brownies in the Cuisinart TOA-60 Convection Toaster Oven Airfryer.

Make smart use of the oven racks that this toaster oven air fryer comes with to your own advantage. While the first position of the rack is for broiling and airfrying food, the second tray position will allow you to toast breads and buns without necessarily burning them in the process.

Starting from broiling chicken, pork, beef and veal, you can even broil your favorite fish with the first rack position of this Cuisinart TOA-60 Convection Toaster Oven Airfryer.

Cooking should be an experience, not a chore! This amazing toaster oven air fryer makes sure that you experience an exceptional moment every time you decide to cook something new and amazing for yourself as well as your loved ones.

Basic Matters That Need Attention

It is a given that you will be required to pay special attention to the Cuisinart TOA-60 Convection Toaster Oven Airfryer during usage and even when it is left idle.

For instance, you will have to make sure that kids or pets do not come in contact with the gadget during its operation, as the product uses a high electricity wattage amount to operate with full power.

Letting children and pets around the equipment during the cooking/baking/broiling or airfrying process could cause unfortunate accidents to take place. If you are going to be using the equipment early in the morning or at night, remember to completely turn the toaster oven airfryer off after usage.

Another matter that needs your attention is to not leave the toaster oven air fryer open with its oven rack outside with the power on. This will not only damage the equipment itself, but can also cause a short circuit or electrical fuse in the power line of your house.

Even though the equipment can turn itself off when left idle for a while, try not to do so by turning it off yourself anyway. This will increase the longevity of the product as well.

Make sure to go through the entire manual instruction guide that is provided with the cCuisinart TOA-60 Convection Toaster Oven Airfryer in order to understand what each part does and how you can take care of the overall equipment.

Using the Cuisinart TOA-60 Convection Toaster Oven Airfryer is not too hard at all, as you can easily understand what each part and function does while making use of the product on a regular basis.

However, we are sure you will find it easier to navigate through the product after reading this cookbook as well as the manual instruction guide that comes with the toaster oven air fryer itself.

Simply Ways to Clean and Maintain the Appliance

Whether it's a traditional toaster oven or a convection one with an airfryer incorporated into the mix, both types of equipment require cleaning and proper maintenance on a regular basis.

Before you start cleaning the product, try to use the equipment regularly to begin with, as that will prevent the gadget from getting rusty or corroded over time.

On top of that, you should refrain from rinsing the entire gadget with buckets of water when cleaning. We know, cleaning certain corners and areas can be pretty hard without water, but you need to still keep it to a minimum.

If usage of water is absolutely necessary, do so with only a soft cloth or a sponge. You should also completely disconnect the equipment from the power supply before introducing any kind of cleansing liquid to it.

Make sure to let the equipment dry out completely before you plug it again for usage.

One simple way to clean and maintain the Cuisinart TOA-60 Convection Toaster Oven Airfryer is by doing it at least once a week. This way, you will be preventing excess dust, gunk and oil from sticking to the internal walls of the toaster oven airfryer.

Getting rid of the oil residue will also be much easier as you will not have to clean through layers and layers of oil and food spills.

To make cleaning even easier, we suggest you to individually wash or rinse the additional parts of the Cuisinart TOA-60 Convection Toaster Oven Airfryer after every use. This means you should take out the trays and additional pans accordingly and clean them right after usage.

Not only will this make your final cleaning process much easier to deal with, but you can also cook something else without wasting too much time.

When cleaning the individual trays and pans, use only soft soap and bristles to scrub with as that will prevent you from peeling the non-stick substance off of the pans and trays.

Chapter 1: Brunches

1.Breakfast Frittata with Spinach and Bacon

Preparation Time: 15 minutes

Cooking Time: 20 minutes

Servings: 3

Ingredients:

- 4 eggs, beaten
- Spinach, chopped
- ½ cup of Cheddar or Swiss cheese
- ¼ pound of sausage of choice, cooked
- 2 tablespoons of red and yellow bell pepper, diced
- 1 pinch of cayenne
- 1 pinch of black pepper
- 1 tablespoon of butter, salted

Method:

1. Combine the sausage, eggs and the veggies with cheese and mix properly after seasoning.
2. Preheat the Cuisinart TOA-60 Convection Toaster Oven Airfryer to 182C or 360F and put the mixture in a bowl or pan spread with butter.
3. Place the bowl or pan with mixture inside the air fryer and set the timer to 18 minutes.
4. Take it out when you notice the frittata has set properly

Serving Suggestion: Garnish with coriander or parsley

Preparation & Cooking Tips: Add more veggies to make it healthier

2. Scotch Eggs

Preparation Time: 15 minutes

Cooking Time: 15 minutes

Servings: 6

Ingredients:
- 1-pound pork sausage
- 6 eggs, hard-boiled and peeled
- 1/3 cup flour
- 2 eggs, beaten
- 1 cup of bread crumbs
- Cooking spray

Method:
1. Evenly divide the pork sausage into 6 portions and make thin patties.
2. In the middle of each patty, place one egg and wrap around the edges.
3. Preheat the Cuisinart TOA-60 Convection Toaster Oven Airfryer to 198C or 390F.
4. Dip each sausage-wrapped egg in flour, then in the beaten egg. Letting the excess egg drip off, roll them in bread crumbs.
5. Spray the basket with cooking spray and place each inside them.
6. Start the air fryer and cook for 12-15 minutes, turning them halfway.
7. Cook until they become brown evenly.

Serving Suggestion: Serve with a dipping sauce.

Preparation & Cooking Tips: Do not overcrowd ; try to cook in batches.

3. Raspberry French Toast

Preparation Time: 20 minutes

Cooking Time: 20 minutes

Servings: 2

Ingredients:

- 2 slices of milk breads, cut into cubes
- ½ cup of frozen raspberries
- 2 eggs
- 2 ounces of cream cheese
- 1 cup whole milk
- 1 tablespoon honey

Method:

1. Place half of the bread cubes in a greased pan, sprinkle with raspberries and cream cheese.
2. Preheat the Cuisinart TOA-60 Convection Toaster Oven Airfryer to 165C or 330F and place the pan.
3. Cook for 12-15 minutes until the top turns golden brown.
4. Cool down the toast to room temperature.

Serving Suggestion: Prepare a raspberry syrup to serve with the toast.

Preparation & Cooking Tips: Add a pinch of cinnamon for flavor.

4. Fried Eggs with Bacon

Preparation Time: 2 minutes

Cooking Time: 10 minutes

Servings: 2

Ingredients:

- 2 eggs
- 1 tablespoon of butter
- 1 ounce of bacon strips
- 1 green onion
- 1 pinch of salt and pepper

Method:

1. Take an aluminum pan to the basket of the air fryer
2. Spread the butter and heat the Cuisinart TOA-60 Convection Toaster Oven Airfryer to 177C or 350F for 1 minute
3. Crack the eggs on the pan for 2 minutes.
4. Broil the bacon strips for half a minute.
5. Plate the fried eggs with the broiled bacon on top.

Serving Suggestion: Serve it with hot sauce.

Preparation & Cooking Tips: Cook the egg and bacon in greased cups.

5. Sausage and Egg Casserole

Preparation Time: 15 minutes

Cooking Time: 15 minutes

Servings: 4

Ingredients:

- 1 pound of Breakfast Sausage, ground
- 4 eggs
- 1 red and 1 green bell pepper
- ¼ cup of sweet onion
- 1 yellow bell pepper
- 1 pinch of salt and pepper

Method:

1. Whisk the eggs and put salt, pepper into the mixture.
2. Mix all the vegetables prepared with the beaten eggs.
3. Preheat the sausage in the Cuisinart TOA-60 Convection Toaster Oven Airfryer at 150C or 300F.
4. Sprinkle the sausage over the casserole egg mixture.
5. Grease a baking dish with oil and pour the mixture in it.
6. Place it in the air fryer and cook at 177C or 350F for 15 minutes.

Serving Suggestion: Serve with some cheese broiled on top.

Preparation & Cooking Tips: Use milk and different kinds of vegetables for a more tasty casserole.

6. Breakfast Burritos

Preparation Time: 20 minutes

Cooking Time: 3 minutes

Servings: 8

Ingredients:

- 1 pound of breakfast sausage
- 1 bell pepper, chopped
- 8 eggs beaten
- 1 teaspoon of sea salt and black pepper
- 8 tortillas
- 2-3 cups of Colby jack cheese, shredded

Method:

1. Cook the sausage on a skillet and stir in bell peppers with it.
2. Melt butter and add the eggs, salt, pepper. Cook them in the Cuisinart TOA-60 Convection Toaster Oven Airfryer for 5 minutes at 149C or 300F.
3. Place the egg and sausage prepared in the air fryer on a tortilla and roll.
4. Preheat the air fryer to 200C or 390F.
5. Place the burritos after spraying slightly with oil and cook for a minute.

Serving Suggestion: Serve with a dipping sauce or ranch dressing.

Preparation & Cooking Tips: Flip the burrito half-way through.

7. Hot Chicken with Waffles

Preparation Time: 20 minutes

Cooking Time: 20 minutes

Servings: 4

Ingredients:

- 4 Chicken thighs, deboned.
- 1 L Milk
- 2 tablespoon of flour
- 1 teaspoon of garlic powder
- 1 teaspoon of paprika
- 1 pinch of cayenne
- 4 eggs
- 1 teaspoon of baking powder

Method:

1. Marinate the chicken with salt, pepper and milk for an hour.
2. Preheat the Cuisinart TOA-60 Convection Toaster Oven Airfryer to 190C or 375F.
3. Dip the chickens in the flour mixture and coat properly.
4. Air fry for 20 minutes.
5. Mix the waffle ingredients and prepare the waffles in the waffle maker.

Serving Suggestion: Serve with some ketchup or garlic mayo with the chicken.

Preparation & Cooking Tips: Marinate the chicken overnight for better taste.You can also use chicken breast for this recipe.

8. Low Carb Sweet Potato Hash Brown

Preparation Time: 10 minutes

Cooking Time: 20 minutes

Servings: 4

Ingredients:

- 4 sweet potatoes, peeled and grated
- 2 garlic cloves
- 1 teaspoon cinnamon
- 1 teaspoon chili
- 1 pinch of salt and pepper
- 1 tablespoon of olive oil

Method:

1. Place the sweet potatoes in cold water and soak them for 20 minutes.
2. Drain them and dry with a paper towel.
3. In a dry bowl, place them and add olive oil with seasoning.
4. Cook in the Cuisinart TOA-60 Convection Toaster Oven Airfryer for 10 minutes at 204C or 400F.
5. Let it cool before serving.

Serving Suggestion: Serve the hash browns with pepper sauce or mayo.

Preparation & Cooking Tips: Check mid-way if the hash browns are crunchy enough. Cook a minute more as air fryers may vary in output

9. Cinnamon Sugary Doughnuts

Preparation Time: 10 minutes

Cooking Time: 10 minutes

Servings: 8

Ingredients:
- ¼ cup of butter, melted
- ¼ cup of sugar, both brown and white.
- 1 package of flaky cookie dough
- ¼ teaspoon of nutmeg
- 1 teaspoon of cinnamon

Method:

1.Combine the sugar with cinnamon and nutmeg; melt the butter and mix it with the combined part in a second bowl.

2.Make the cookie dough into doughnut shape by cutting in centers.

3.Preheat the Cuisinart TOA-60 Convection Toaster Oven Airfryer to 177C or 350F and cook them for 3 minutes.

4.Dip them in the sugary syrup mix and serve.

Serving Suggestion: Serve with chocolate syrup or Nutella.

Preparation & Cooking Tips: Rest the cookie dough for longer for better texture.

10.Crunchy Sushi Rolls

Preparation Time: 20 minutes

Cooking Time: 10 minutes

Servings: 3

Ingredients:

- 1 cup of kale, chopped
- ½ teaspoon of rice vinegar
- ¾ teaspoon soy sauce
- ¼ teaspoon of ginger powder
- 1/8 spoon of garlic powder
- ¾ teaspoon of sesame oil
- 1 cup of precooked white or brown rice
- 1 cup of panko breadcrumbs

Method:

1. Combine the kale, sesame oil and vinegar to make the kale salad.
2. Add the seasoning to the salad and stir in sesame seeds.
3. On a sheet of nori, place the rice and spread it evenly. Make sure to wet the fingertips, or else the rice will stick to your hands.
4. Add the kale salad on top of the rice and some avocado slices.
5. Roll them and seal carefully.
6. Coat the sushi rolls in panko breadcrumbs and place them in an air fryer basket.
7. Air fry the sushi rolls for 10 minutes at 200C or 390F in the Cuisinart TOA-60 Convection Toaster Oven Airfryer.
8. Cool them and slice in small bites.

Serving Suggestion: Drizzle over some sriracha sauce or mayo on top of the sushi rolls before serving.

Preparation & Cooking Tips: Prepare the rice beforehand and do not overcook in the fryer.

Chapter 2: Beef, Pork, & Lamb

1. Beef Zucchini Boats

Preparation Time: 10 minutes

Cooking Time: 15 minutes

Serving: 3

Ingredients:

- 3 medium-sized zucchinis
- 250 grams ground beef
- ½ cup onion, diced
- 1 teaspoon paprika
- 3/4 cup marinara sauce
- 1/2 teaspoon Italian herbs

Method:

- Choose bake setting in Cuisinart TOA-60 Convection Toaster Oven Airfryerand preheat to 180C or 350F.
- Wash the zucchinis and cut it in half. Scoop all the flesh out.
- Add all the spices into the ground beef and mix it well.
- Fill the boats with beef mixture and put shredded cheese on top.
- Bake for 15 minutes.

Serving Suggestion: Serve while it's piping hot.

Preparation and Cooking Tips: You can also use bell peppers for this recipe.

2. Beef Steak Bites

Preparation Time: 5 minutes

Cooking Time: 15 minutes

Serving: 5

Ingredients:

- 1 lb. sirloin steaks cut into cubes
- 2 tablespoons melted butter
- 1 teaspoon Worcestershire sauce
- Salt and pepper to taste
- 1/2 teaspoon garlic powder

Method:

1. Rinse and pat the steak cubes dry.
2. Coat the steak cubes with melted butter and Worcestershire sauce and season it well with garlic powder, salt, and pepper.
3. Preheat the Cuisinart TOA-60 Convection Toaster Oven Airfryer at 180C or 350F and bake the steak for 15 minutes.

Serving Suggestion: Garnish with some fresh parsley on top.

Preparation and Cooking Tips: If you want your steaks to be well-done, cook for an extra 5 minutes.

3. Greek Beef Tortellini

Preparation Time: 15 minutes

Cooking Time: 30 minutes

Serving: 5

Ingredients:

20 ounces frozen cheese tortellini
- 1 lb. ground beef
- 1 large zucchini, red onion, and tomato
- 3 cups marinara sauce
- 1 cup of water
- Salt and pepper to taste
- 1/2 cup feta cheese
- 1 cup white wine

Method:
1. Defrost the tortellini and meanwhile chop up the veggies.
2. In a large skillet combine all the ingredients and give it a good stir.
3. Choose the bake setting in Cuisinart TOA-60 Convection Toaster Oven Airfryer and preheat it to 149C or 300F.
4. Place the skillet in the air fryer and bake for 30 minutes.

Serving Suggestion: Sprinkle some fresh basil before serving.

Preparation and Cooking Tips: You can also use water instead of white wine.

4. Skillet Beef Casserole

Preparation Time: 5 minutes

Cooking Time: 30 minutes

Serving: 5

Ingredients:

- 1 lb ground beef
- 3 tablespoons taco seasoning
- ½ cup enchilada sauce
- ¾ cup of rice
- 2 oz cream cheese
- ½ cup sweet corn
- ½ cup shredded mozzarella

Method:

1. In an oven-safe skillet, place all the ingredients and give it a good mix.
2. Choose bake setting in Cuisinart TOA-60 Convection Toaster Oven Airfryer and preheat to 149C or 300F.
3. Bake it for 25 minutes.
4. Top the skillet with the shredded mozzarella.
5. Set the air fryer to its broil setting.
6. Broil for a few minutes until the cheese bubbles.

Serving Suggestion: Garnish with some fresh cilantro, if desired.

Preparation and Cooking Tips: If you want, you can exclude rice from the recipe.

5. Lamb Hotpot

Preparation Time: 5 minutes

Cooking Time: 30 minutes

Serving: 5

Ingredients:

- 500 g lamb leg cubes
- 2 large carrots, cubed
- 3 large potatoes, sliced
- 1 cup lamb stock
- Salt and pepper to taste
- 1 tablespoon olive oil

Method:

1. Choose the bake setting and preheat the Cuisinart TOA-60 Convection Toaster Oven Airfryer to 180C or 350F.
2. Grease a large skillet with oil and place all the ingredients in it.
3. Cover the skillet with a lid and bake for 40 minutes.

Serving Suggestion: To add creaminess, serve with a dollop of sour cream.

Preparation and Cooking Tips: Put ingredients that take a bit longer to cook, such as potatoes, to the pan first.

6. Rosemary Lamb Chop

Preparation Time: 5 minutes

Cooking Time: 15 minutes

Serving: 5

Ingredients:
- 12 lamb chops
- 3 tablespoon rosemary, chopped
- 3 cloves garlic, finely chopped
- 2 tbsp olive oil
- ¼ tablespoon salt
- ¼ tablespoon ground black pepper

Method:
1. Mix all the ingredients and rub it on the lamb chops.
2. Place the chops on a large cast-iron skillet.
3. Set the Cuisinart TOA-60 Convection Toaster Oven Airfryer to its broil setting.
4. Broil for about 10-15 minutes.

Serving Suggestion: For an extra zing of flavor, serve with some lime juice on top.

Preparation and Cooking Tips: If you don't have fresh rosemary at home, use the ground one instead.

7. Slow Roast Lamb

Preparation Time: 5 minutes

Cooking Time: 60 minutes

Serving: 6

Ingredients:
- 1 lb. boneless lamb shoulder
- 1 lb. potatoes
- 3 tablespoon olive oil
- 3 cloves garlic, minced
- 2 tablespoon Italian ground herbs
- Kosher salt
- Freshly ground pepper

Method:
- Tie up the lamb shoulder using a twine.
- Choose the bake setting and preheat the Cuisinart TOA-60 Convection Toaster Oven Airfryer to 180C or 350F.
- Combine all the seasonings and rub it all over the lamb.
- Grease a large pan with oil and place the lamb and potatoes on it.
- Bake for an hour.

Serving Suggestion: Allow the lamb to rest for 15 minutes before serving.

Preparation and Cooking Tips: Choose a fattier joint of the shoulder for extra juicy and tender meat.

8. Greek Lamb Pasticcio

Preparation Time: 15 minutes

Cooking Time: 45 minutes

Serving: 3

Ingredients:
- 400g minced lamb
- 400g tomato puree
- 200g dried macaroni
- 3 tablespoon Mediterranean seasoning
- 1 tablespoon dried oregano
- 1 cup of water
- 150 ml Greek yogurt
- 1 cup feta cheese

Method:
- Choose the bake setting and heat the Cuisinart TOA-60 Convection Toaster Oven Airfryer to 82C or 180F.
- Place all the ingredients except the yogurt and cheese on a large pan. Give it a good mix.
- Place in the fryer and bake it for 30 minutes.
- Top the pan with yogurt and feta cheese.
- Broil it for another 15 minutes.

Serving Suggestion: Sprinkle with some extra oregano before serving.

Preparation and Cooking Tips: For a creamier result, add some cream cheese to the recipe.

9. Baked Pork Pot Stickers

Preparation Time: 15 minutes

Cooking Time: 15 minutes

Serving: 3

Ingredients:

- 300 gm minced pork meat
- 15 wonton wrappers
- 1 cup green onion, chopped
- 1 tablespoon ginger and garlic paste
- 3 tablespoon soy sauce
- Salt and pepper to taste

Method:

- Choose the bake setting in Cuisinart TOA-60 Convection Toaster Oven Airfryer and preheat to 218C or 425F.
- In a bowl, combine the minced pork and spices together.
- Place the wrappers onto a dry surface and place a generous amount of filling onto the center of each wrapper and fold the edges.
- Bake the wontons for 15 minutes until golden brown.

Serving Suggestion: Serve with a dipping sauce of your choice.

Preparation and Cooking Tips: Don't overcrowd the pan if you want the potstickers to be crispy.

10. Pork Tenderloin

Preparation Time: 5 minutes

Cooking Time: 30 minutes

Serving: 6

Ingredients:

- 1lb pork tenderloin
- Salt and pepper to taste
- 1 tablespoon garlic and onion powder
- 1 tablespoon Italian seasoning

Method:

- Choose the broil setting in Cuisinart TOA-60 Convection Toaster Oven Airfryer.
- Season the tenderloin as desired and place it in a roasting pan.
- Broil for 30 minutes.

Serving Suggestion: Serve with some roasted veggies on the side.

Preparation and Cooking Tips: Make sure the center of the tenderloin doesn't get cooked past 65C or 150F for a tender outcome.

Chapter 3: Fish & Seafood

1. Black Cod with Black Bean Sauce

Preparation Time: 25 minutes

Cooking Time: 17 minutes

Servings: 2

Ingredients:
- 1 lb. piece of black cod, ½ inch thick
- 1 tablespoon garlic, minced
- 1 tablespoon soy sauce
- 1 teaspoon brown sugar
- 1 teaspoon salt and pepper
- ½ Black Beans, fermented
- ½ sesame oil

Method:
1. Marinate the black cod with garlic, soy sauce, salt and pepper.
2. Rest it for 10 minutes in a bowl.
3. Heat the Cuisinart TOA-60 Convection Toaster Oven Airfryer to 180C or 350F.
4. Place the fish in the air fryer basket and cook it for 15 minutes at 350 degrees F.
5. Prepare the black bean sauce by mixing the fermented black bean, water, soy sauce and sesame oil.
6. Take the cod fish out of the air fryer and plate it up. Drizzle the black bean sauce generously.

Serving Suggestion: Garnish with some cucumber salad or cilantro.

Preparation & Cooking Tips: Rest the marinated fish overnight for better taste.

2. Crispy Salmon and Crab Fish Cakes

Preparation Time: 15 minutes

Cooking Time: 14 minutes

Servings: 5

Ingredients:

- 1 can of salmon flakes
- 1 can of crab meat
- 1 large egg, beaten
- 4 tablespoon of mayonnaise
- ½ teaspoon of garlic and onion powder
- ½ teaspoon of salt and pepper
- ½ teaspoon of paprika
- 1 cup of panko
- 1 teaspoon Worcestershire sauce

Method:

1. Mix all the ingredients in a bowl and make small patties of around 10 portions.
2. Preheat the Cuisinart TOA-60 Convection Toaster Oven Airfryer at 204C or 400F for about 3-4 minutes.
3. Brush the fish cakes with oil or clarified butter and place them in the air fryer.
4. Cook the fish cakes for 8 minutes and flip halfway.

Serving Suggestion: Serve it with a smoky dipping sauce or a side salad.

Preparation & Cooking Tips: Add herbs such as dill or cilantro for freshness.

3. Fish en Papillote

Preparation Time: 10 minutes

Cooking Time: 15 minutes

Servings: 2

Ingredients:

- 2.5 oz. Cod Fillets
- ½ cup carrots, julienned
- ½ cup fennel, julienned
- 2 tablespoon of butter, salted
- ½ cup of red pepper, sliced
- 1 tablespoon of salt
- 1 tablespoon of lemon juice
- ½ teaspoon of black pepper
- 1 tablespoon of oil

Method:

1. Combine the butter, salt, lemon juice to make a creamy sauce. Add the vegetables prepared beforehand.
2. Prepare the fish fillets by spraying them with oil and seasoning them on both sides.
3. Take a parchment paper and cut in half, place the fish fillets and veggies on them and securely pack them.
4. Place the packets in the air fryer basket and set the Cuisinart TOA-60 Convection Toaster Oven Airfryer to 180C or 350F for 15 minutes.

Serving Suggestion: You can serve with some fresh dill or parsley.

Preparation & Cooking Tips: Use dried or fresh tarragon for a boost in taste.

4.   Classic Fish and Chips

Preparation Time: 15 minutes

Cooking Time: 25 minutes

Servings: 4

Ingredients:
- 1 lb. potatoes
- 2 tablespoon of oil
- ¼ teaspoon pepper
- ¼ teaspoon salt
- 1/3 cup flour, all-purpose
- 1 large egg
- 2 tablespoons water
- 1 cup of cornflakes, crushed
- 1 pound of cod or haddock

Method:
1. Peel and cut potatoes lengthwise and toss them with salt and pepper.
2. Wash the fish fillets and season them.
3. Preheat the Cuisinart TOA-60 Convection Toaster Oven Airfryer to 204C or 400F.
4. Put the potatoes in the basket and fry them until golden and crispy.
5. Mix flour, pepper and salt. Whisk an egg with some water in another bowl.
6. Dip the fish in the egg mixture first, then on the flour and cornflakes.
7. Remove the fries from the basket and place the fish fillets one by one, cook them for 8-10 minutes.

Serving Suggestion: Serve with the delicious tartar sauce.

Preparation & Cooking Tips: Turn halfway during the cooking and check carefully to avoid overcooking.

5. White Fish with Garlic and Lemon

Preparation Time: 5 minutes

Cooking Time: 12 minutes

Servings: 2

Ingredients:

- 12 ounces of tilapia fillets or any other white fish
- 1 lemon, cut into wedges
- ½ teaspoon garlic powder
- ½ teaspoon of lemon pepper and onion powder
- 1 teaspoon of salt and black pepper

Method:

1. Preheat the Cuisinart TOA-60 Convection Toaster Oven Airfryer to 182C or 360F for 5-7 minutes.
2. Wash the fish fillets and pat dry them. Spray some oil and add the seasonings at both sides.
3. Take the air fryer basket and place the fishes on it.
4. Air fry the fish for 7-12 minutes until it can be easily flaked with a spoon.
5. Place lemon wedges on the fish to infuse flavor.

Serving Suggestion: Serve with fresh chopped parsley and lemon wedges.

Preparation & Cooking Tips: Use perforated air fryer basket baking paper to place the fish inside the basket.

6. Korean Spicy Croaker Fish

Preparation Time: 10 minutes

Cooking Time: 10 minutes

Servings: 3

Ingredients:

- 6 medium sized yellow croaker fish
- 1 tablespoon of rice vinegar
- 1 ½ teaspoon of gochujang or Korean red pepper paste
- 2 tablespoon honey
- ½ teaspoon of soy sauce

Method:

1. Marinate the fish using the rice vinegar and rest it for 5 minutes. Pat dry it with a paper towel gently.
2. Mix gochujang, honey and soy sauce.
3. Line the air fryer basket of Cuisinart TOA-60 Convection Toaster Oven Airfryer with a lightly greased foil.
4. Make a few slices on the fish on each side for full flavors.
5. Air fry the fish at 204C or 400F for 5 minutes on each side.
6. Turn the fish halfway through and brush sauce on it.

Serving Suggestion: Serve with rice and kimchi with a drizzle of hot sauce.

Preparation & Cooking Tips: You can use corn syrup instead of honey and rice wine instead of rice vinegar.

7.   Halibut with Parmesan Sauce

Preparation Time: 15 minutes

Cooking Time: 10 minutes

Servings: 4

Ingredients:
- 4 halibut fillets
- 4 garlic cloves
- ½ teaspoon salt
- ¼ teaspoon of black pepper
- 1 tablespoon of butter, unsalted
- ¼ teaspoon of white wine
- ½ teaspoon of chicken stock
- Lemon zest
- 1 oz. Parmesan cheese

Method:
1. Preheat the Cuisinart TOA-60 Convection Toaster Oven Airfryer to 204C or 400F.
2. Mix salt, pepper and garlic cloves and rub the mixture on a washed and dry halibut fish.
3. Prepare the sauce by adding butter in a pan. Add flour and garlic, sauté until brown.
4. Slowly add white wine and chicken stock; bring it to boil. Season it properly and simmer until you get a thick texture.
5. Place the fish in the air fryer basket after spraying oil in it.
6. Air fry the fish for 5-12 minutes. Transfer the fish onto a serving plate.

Serving Suggestion: Serve with some rice or quinoa.

Preparation & Cooking Tips: Check if the fish has cooked properly by testing the temperature inside the fish.

8. Hoisin Glazed Salmon

Preparation Time: 5 minutes

Cooking Time: 10 minutes

Servings: 2

Ingredients:

- 2.5 Oz of Salmon fillets, skin on
- 1 pinch of kosher salt
- 1 pinch of black pepper
- 1 tablespoon of hoisin sauce
- 1 teaspoon soy sauce
- 1 teaspoon of brown sugar
- 1 clove garlic, minced
- ½ teaspoon of rice wine
- ½ teaspoon of sesame seeds

Method:

1. Preheat the Cuisinart TOA-60 Convection Toaster Oven Airfryer to 204C or 400 F for 7 minutes
2. Generously season the salmon fish with salt and pepper.
3. Whisk together hoisin,soy sauce, brown sugar, garlic, ginger and vinegar; brush the mixture on the salmon.
4. Place the salmon on the air fryer basket and cook for 10 minutes, until it reaches 63C or 145F.
5. Sprinkle sesame seeds and serve it on a plate.

Serving Suggestion: Serve it with some stir fried veggies.

Preparation & Cooking Tips: You can use lemon juice instead of vinegar.

9.   Baked Salmon with Garlic

Preparation Time: 10 minutes

Cooking Time: 10 minutes

Servings: 2

Ingredients:

- 6 oz. salmon fillets with skin
- ¼ teaspoon of lemon pepper seasoning
- 1/8 teaspoon of dried parsley
- ½ teaspoon of garlic, minced
- 1 tablespoon melted butter
- Lemon slices

Method:

1. Preheat the Cuisinart TOA-60 Convection Toaster Oven Airfryer to 202C or 396F.
2. Mix the melted butter and garlic in a bowl.
3. Rinse the salmon fillets and pat dry. Brush the butter mixture and seasonings.
4. Spray the basket with cooking spray and place the salmon fillets skin down.
5. Cook the fish for 8-10 minutes and rest it for 2 minutes.

Serving Suggestion: Serve with some cooked white rice or mashed potatoes.

Preparation & Cooking Tips: Try to place a baking sheet and place the fish fillets on it to avoid sticking.

10. Lobster Tails in Lemon-Garlic Butter

Preparation Time: 10 minutes

Cooking Time: 10 minutes

Servings: 2

Ingredients:

- 2 lobster tails
- 1 teaspoon lemon zest
- 1 clove garlic, grated
- 3 tablespoon butter
- ½ tablespoon of salt and pepper

Method:

1. Butterfly the lobster tails by cutting through the meat till the bottom shell.
2. Melt butter on a pan and add lemon zest and garlic until soft.
3. Brush butter on the tails. Season with salt and pepper.
4. Cook in the Cuisinart TOA-60 Convection Toaster Oven Airfryer for 5 to 7 minutes, at 193-198C or 380-390F.
5. Drizzle the butter from the pan onto the fish and serve.

Serving Suggestion: Garnish with parsley and a mashed potato side.

Preparation & Cooking Tips: You can use both fresh and frozen lobsters ; thaw the latter properly.

Chapter 4: Chicken & Poultry

1. Broiled Lemon Pepper Chicken

Preparation Time: 10 minutes
Cooking Time: 10 minutes
Servings: 4
Ingredients:
- 4 chicken breast pieces
- 2½ tbsp. olive oil
- 4 cloves minced garlic
- 2 tbsp. lemon-pepper
- 2 tbsp. paprika
- 2 tbsp. kosher salt
- ½ cup chicken broth
- Lemon, sliced into thin rounds

Method:
1. Choose the broiler setting.
2. Preheat the Cuisinart TOA-60 Convection Toaster Oven Airfryer to 100C or 212F.
3. Brush the chicken breast pieces with olive oil, and sprinkle the seasonings on both sides.
4. Place the chicken breast pieces into a well-greased broiler pan.
5. Pour the chicken broth, tack on the sliced lemon.
6. Set the pan into the preheated broiler. After about 5 minutes, flip the chicken pieces and let them cook for another 5 minutes.

Serving Suggestions: Serve by topping some parsley leaves.
Preparation & Cooking Tips: You can add on other spices of your choice.

2. Chicken Loaf

Preparation Time: 15 minutes

Cooking Time: 50 minutes

Servings: 6

Ingredients:

- 500g ground chicken
- 1 cup onion, diced
- 1 egg
- ½ cup stuffing mix crumbs
- 2 tbsp. barbeque sauce
- 2 tbsp. tomato ketchup
- Garlic pepper and salt to taste
- ½ cup parmesan cheese, grated

Method:

1. Preheat the Cuisinart TOA-60 Convection Toaster Oven Airfryer to 190C or 375F.
2. Combine all the ingredients into a bowl and mix.
3. Pour the mixture in a bread loaf pan.
4. Bake for 50 minutes.

Serving Suggestions: Serve sliced chicken loaf with mint or coriander chutney.

Preparation & Cooking Tips: Brush the raw loaf top with egg wash to get a golden crust.

3. Baked BBQ Chicken

Preparation Time: 10 minutes

Cooking Time: 35 minutes

Servings: 2

Ingredients:

- 4 chicken legs
- ½ cup barbeque sauce
- ¼ cup marinade sauce
- Pepper and salt to taste

Method:

1. Rub the chicken legs with the marinade sauce.
2. Keep in the fridge for at least 40 minutes.
3. Place the legs in a broiler pan.
4. Brush with barbeque sauce.
5. Sprinkle the pepper and salt.
6. Choose the broiler setting in Cuisinart TOA-60 Convection Toaster Oven Airfryer.
7. Cook at 190C or 375F for 35 minutes.

Serving Suggestions: Serve with mashed potato and stir fried veggies.

Preparation & Cooking Tips: For the best result, keep it marinated overnight.

4. Sesame Chicken Toast

Preparation Time: 20 minutes

Cooking Time: 15 minutes

Servings: 4

Ingredients:

- 500g chicken mince
- ½ cup white sesame seeds
- 2 tbsp. five-spice powder
- Pepper and salt to taste
- 8 slices thin sliced bread

Method:

1. Put chicken mince and spice powder into a food processor.
2. Make a thick paste with necessary whirls.
3. Smear the mixture onto the bread evenly.
4. Top them with sesame seeds.
5. Add to the Cuisinart TOA-60 Convection Toaster Oven Airfryer.
6. Set it to 190C or 375F
7. Cook for 15 minutes.

Serving Suggestions: Serve with mustard and tomato ketchup.

Preparation & Cooking Tips: You can cut the toast into whatever shapes you like.

5. Baked Chicken Wings

Preparation Time: 10 minutes
Cooking Time: 40 minutes
Servings: 2

Ingredients:

- · 8 chicken wings
- · 2 tbsp. olive oil
- · 1 tbsp. garlic powder
- · 1½ tbsp. chili powder
- · ½ tbsp. soy sauce
- · Pepper and salt to taste

Method:

1. Preheat the Cuisinart TOA-60 Convection Toaster Oven Airfryer to 185C or 365F.
2. Combine the spices in a bowl, add soy sauce and olive oil.
3. With a spoon swirl them together into a paste.
4. Coat the wings with the made spice rub.
5. Place them in the middle rack and let them bake in the preheated oven for 40 minutes.

Serving Suggestions: Serve with mashed potatoes and mustard.

Preparation & Cooking Tips: If you want the chicken wings to be crispy, toss them in hot oil for 2-3 minutes before rubbing the spice paste.

6. Crispy Chicken Tenders

Preparation Time: 5 minutes

Cooking Time: 30 minutes

Servings: 4

Ingredients:
- 12 raw chicken wedges
- 2 eggs
- 1 tbsp. olive oil
- 1 tbsp. kosher salt
- ½ cup seasoned breadcrumbs
- Pepper to taste

Method:
1. Preheat the Cuisinart TOA-60 Convection Toaster Oven Airfryer to 190C or 375F
2. Rub the chicken pieces with pepper and salt.
3. Dip each piece into the beaten egg mixture, and coat with breadcrumbs.
4. Place them in the preheated air fryer in turn.
5. Cook for about 30 minutes.

Serving Suggestions: Serve with ketchup to your liking.

Preparation & Cooking Tips: Add in panko if you like to have it with more crisp.

7. Turkey Burgers

Preparation Time: 10 minutes

Cooking Time: 15 minutes

Servings: 2

Ingredients:

- 1 cup ground turkey
- 1 jalapeno, diced
- 2 raw onion rings
- Burger seasonings
- Mayonnaise and ketchup to your liking
- 1 burger bun

Method:

1. Preheat the Cuisinart TOA-60 Convection Toaster Oven Airfryer to 230C or 450F.
2. Mix the ground turkey, jalapeno, and seasonings well.
3. Shape it as a burger patties.
4. Cook it for 15 minutes.
5. Wrap it with a bun adding mayonnaise, ketchup, and onion rings.

Serving Suggestions: Serve with adding sliced cheese.

Preparation & Cooking Tips: Toast the bun before tucking the patties.

8. Chicken Parmesan

Preparation Time: 20 minutes

Cooking Time: 30 minutes

Servings: 4

Ingredients:

- 4 boneless chicken breast
- 1 tbsp. olive oil
- ½ cup mozzarella cheese, grated
- ½ cup provolone cheese, grated
- 2 tbsp. tomato sauce
- Pepper and salt to taste

Method:

1. Pat chicken pieces dry, dust the pepper and salt.
2. Brush tomato sauce and olive oil on both sides.
3. Top all the cheeses in turn.
4. Add to the Cuisinart TOA-60 Convection Toaster Oven Airfryer.
5. Choose grill setting.
6. Cook at 230C or 450Ffor 30 minutes.

Serving Suggestions: Spread some basil on top and serve with white noodles.

Preparation & Cooking Tips: You can also add parmesan cheese to make it more cheesy.

9. Chicken Patties

Preparation Time: 30 minutes

Cooking Time: 15 minutes

Servings: 5

Ingredients:

- 2 cups ground chicken
- 1 cup chopped onion
- 1 egg
- 4 tbsp. vegetable oil
- 2 tbsp. parsley flakes
- 2 tbsp mayonnaise
- Black pepper and sea-salt to taste
- 1 cup all-purpose flour

Method:

1. Preheat the Cuisinart TOA-60 Convection Toaster Oven Airfryer to 200C or 400F.
2. Combine all the ingredients and mix well.
3. Make a ball-like shape.
4. Coat a thick layer of flour.
5. Place them in the air fryer pan.
6. Cook for 15 minutes.

Serving Suggestions: Serve by sprinkling some parsley flakes on top.

Preparation & Cooking Tips: You can make the patties into any shape to make it more fun for kids.

10. Baked Chicken Cacciatore

Preparation Time: 20 minutes

Cooking Time: 45 minutes

Servings: 2

Ingredients:

- 150g cubed boneless chicken
- ½ cup chopped onion
- 1 bell pepper, minced
- 2 tomatoes, diced
- 2 tbsp. tomato paste
- 2 tbsp. red wine
- ½ cup basil, shredded
- ¼ cup rosemary, shredded
- 1 tbsp. Italian cacciatore seasoning

Method:

1. Mix the cubed chicken with all the ingredients.
2. Pour them into a baking pan.
3. Cook at 200C or 400F for 45 minutes in the Cuisinart TOA-60 Convection Toaster Oven Airfryer.

Serving Suggestions: Serve with polenta or rustic bread.

Preparation & Cooking Tips: Marinate the chicken cubes for 30 minutes to have a more flavorful outcome.

Chapter 5: Vegan & Vegetarian

1. Broccoli Gnocchi Bake

Preparation Time: 15 minutes

Cooking Time: 30 minutes

Serving: 5

Ingredients:

- 100g spinach
- 3 cup cubed broccoli florets
- 500gm ready-made gnocchi
- 1 cup grated parmesan
- 1 tbsp. olive oil
- 2 tbsp. plain flour
- 300ml milk

Method:

1. Choose the bake setting in Cuisinart TOA-60 Convection Toaster Oven Airfryer and preheat to 120C or 250F.
2. Combine all the ingredients in a large pan and mix it well.
3. Top it with the grated parmesan and bake for 30 minutes.

Serving Suggestions: Serve with some extra parmesan on top.

Preparation and Cooking Tips: You can also use cauliflower for this recipe.

2. Maple Baked Beans

Preparation Time: 60 minutes

Cooking Time: 30 minutes

Serving: 5

Ingredients:
- 1 lb. dried beans
- 1 cup water
- 1 cup maple syrup
- Salt and pepper to taste
- 1/3 cup barbecue sauce
- ½ cup ketchup

Method:
1. Soak the beans in cold water for an hour.
2. Choose the air fry setting in Cuisinart TOA-60 Convection Toaster Oven Airfryer and preheat to 150C or 300F.
3. In a large dish, combine beans with all the ingredients.
4. Cook for 30 minutes, stirring occasionally.

Serving Suggestions: Garnish with freshly chopped parsley.

Preparation and Cooking Tips: For the best result, soak the beans overnight.

3. Baked Apple

Preparation Time: 5 minutes

Cooking Time: 20 minutes

Serving: 5

Ingredients:

- 5 large apples
- 1/4 cup brown sugar
- 1 tbsp. melted butter
- 1 tbsp. cinnamon
- A pinch of salt

Method:

1. Choose the bake setting in Cuisinart TOA-60 Convection Toaster Oven Airfryer and preheat the fryer to 180C or 350F.
2. Mix all the dry ingredients and butter until it creates a smooth paste.
3. Create holes in the apples using a fork and rub the paste all over the apples.
4. Bake for 20 minutes.

Serving Suggestions: Serve with a dollop of ice cream on top.

Preparation and Cooking Tips: Create holes on the apples using a fork before rubbing the paste.

4. Zucchini Bread

Preparation Time: 15 minutes

Cooking Time: 60 minutes

Serving: 6

Ingredients:

- 1 cup shredded zucchini
- ½ cup pumpkin puree
- 1/2 cup brown sugar
- 2 cups all-purpose flour
- 1 flax egg
- ½ cup soy milk
- 60ml coconut oil

Method:

1. Choose the bake setting in Cuisinart TOA-60 Convection Toaster Oven Airfryer and preheat the fryer to 180C or 350F.
2. Combine all the ingredients and mix together.
3. Grease and loaf pan with oil and place a parchment paper on it.
4. Pour the batter into the loaf pan.
5. Bake for 60 minutes.

Serving Suggestions: Serve with some pistachios on top.

Preparation and Cooking Tips: Allow the bread to cool before slicing.

5. Cauliflower Pasta Bake

Preparation Time: 15 minutes

Cooking Time: 45 minutes

Serving: 6

Ingredients:

- 3 cup cauliflower, cubed
- 15 ounces macaroni
- 6 cloves garlic, minced
- 1/2 cup cashews
- Salt and pepper to taste
- 3 tbsp. nutritional yeast
- 1 cup bread crumb

Method:

1. Choose the broil setting of the Cuisinart TOA-60 Convection Toaster Oven Airfryer.
2. Place the ingredients in a dish and top it with nutritional yeast and bread crumbs.
3. Cook for 45 minutes.

Serving Suggestions: Serve while it's piping hot with some more nutritional yeast on top.

Preparation and Cooking Tips: If you're not a big fan of nutritional yeast, use vegan cheese instead.

6. Roasted Cheese Cauliflower

Preparation Time: 15 minutes

Cooking Time: 50 minutes

Serving: 3

Ingredients:

- 1 whole cauliflower, stem trimmed
- 3 tbsp. olive oil
- 1 cup marinara sauce
- 1 cup shredded mozzarella
- 1 cup parmesan
- Freshly ground pepper

Method:

1. Choose the air fry setting in Cuisinart TOA-60 Convection Toaster Oven Airfryer and preheat the fryer to 230C or 450F.
2. Soak the cauliflower in hot water for 10 minutes.
3. Brush the oil, marinara all over it, and top it with cheese and pepper.
4. Cook for 50 minutes.

Serving Suggestion: Serve it hot with some garlic aioli on the side.

Preparation and Cooking Tips: You can replace cauliflower with broccoli if you want.

7. Baked Fruit Crumble

Preparation Time: 5 minutes

Cooking Time: 15 minutes

Serving: 3

Ingredients:

- 3 cups of fruits, chopped
- 1 cup rolled oats
- 1 tbsp. brown sugar
- ½ tbsp. cinnamon
- 1 tbsp. agave syrup

Method:

1. Choose the air fry setting in Cuisinart TOA-60 Convection Toaster Oven Airfryer and preheat to 180C or 350F.
2. Combine the oats, sugar, cinnamon, and agave in a bowl.
3. Place the oat mixture over the chopped fruits in another bowl.
4. Bake for 15 minutes.

Serving Suggestion: Drizzle some chocolate syrup on top before serving.

Preparation and Cooking Tips: To add a pop of color, add multiple fruits to the recipe.

8. Peanut Butter Cookies

Preparation Time: 15 minutes

Cooking Time: 45 minutes

Serving: 3

Ingredients:

- 1 cup unsalted peanut butter
- 2 cup all flour
- ½ cup brown sugar
- ½ cup almond milk
- ½ tbsp. baking powder

Method:

1. Choose the bake setting and preheat the Cuisinart TOA-60 Convection Toaster Oven Airfryer to 180C or 350F.
2. In a large bowl, add peanut butter, sugar, milk and mix until smooth.
3. Gradually add in flour and baking powder until it forms into a cookie dough.
4. Scoop out the cookie dough and give it a cookie shape.
5. Bake for 45 minutes.

Serving Suggestion: Let the cookies cool down a bit before serving.

Preparation and Cooking Tips: To take the recipe to a next level, add some chocolate chips to it.

9. Black Bean Brownies

Preparation Time: 10 minutes

Cooking Time: 30 minutes

Serving: 6

Ingredients:
- 2 cup ground black beans
- 2 flax eggs
- 1 cup of sugar
- ½ cup of cocoa powder
- 3 tbsp. coconut oil
- 1 tbsp. baking powder

Method:
1. Choose the bake setting and preheat the Cuisinart TOA-60 Convection Toaster Oven Airfryer to 150C or 300F.
2. In a large pan, whisk flax eggs, sugar, and oil until creamy.
3. Gradually add and mix the bean, flour, baking powder, and cocoa.
4. Pour the batter into a greased muffin pan.
5. Bake for 30 minutes.

Serving Suggestion: Serve with some walnuts or pecans on top.

Preparation and Cooking Tips: If you want your cookies to be on the fudgier side, cook 5 minutes less.

10. Vegan Mac and Cheese

Preparation Time: 15 minutes

Cooking Time: 20 minutes

Serving: 5

Ingredients:

- 1 cup cashew
- 1 cup water
- 15 ounces Elbow pasta, boiled
- 1 tsp. paprika
- 1 cup nutritional yeast
- Salt and pepper to taste

Method:

1. Choose a baking setting in Cuisinart TOA-60 Convection Toaster Oven Airfryer and preheat to 180C or 350F.
2. In a mixer, blend all the ingredients except pasta and blend until smooth.
3. In a large bowl, place the pasta and pour the cashew sauce over it.
4. Bake for 20 minutes.

Serving Suggestion: Serve piping hot with some vegan chili mayo.

Preparation and Cooking Tips: For an extra silky sauce, soak the cashews overnight.

Chapter 6: Baking Recipes

1. Baked Mozzarella Sticks

Preparation Time: 15 minutes

Cooking Time: 5 minutes

Servings: 6

Ingredients:

- 6 frozen mozzarella string cheese sticks
- 1 egg, beaten
- 1 cup flour
- 1 cup seasoned bread crumbs

Method:

1. Cut the cheese sticks into half.
2. Dip each piece into the bowl of flour, beaten egg, and breadcrumbs in turn and toss to coat on all sides.
3. Arrange them sidewise in a baking pan.
4. Bake at 200C or 400F for 5 minutes in the Cuisinart TOA-60 Convection Toaster Oven Airfryer.

Serving Suggestions: Sprinkle pepper on top and serve with ketchup to your liking.

Preparation & Cooking Tips: To add a zesty kick, dip it into Italian seasoning before baking.

2. Blackberry Pie

Preparation Time: 20 minutes

Cooking Time: 35 minutes

Servings: 8

Ingredients:
- 4 cups blackberries, pressed
- 1 cup sugar
- ½ cup tapioca
- 3 tbsp. butter
- Store-bought pie crust

Method:
1. Boil the berries with sugar and tapioca.
2. Stir until the berries burst and the mixture turns into a thick paste.
3. Fill the centre of a pie crust with the made paste, dot with butter.
4. Roll out the edge of the crust to cover the filling and flute the edge.
5. Bake at 200C or 400F for 35 minutes in the Cuisinart TOA-60 Convection Toaster Oven Airfryer.

Serving Suggestions: Serve with whipped cream on top.

Preparation & Cooking Tips: You can also use whipped cream as filling.

3. Cheese Stuffed Baked Potatoes

Preparation Time: 3 minutes

Cooking Time: 5 minutes

Servings: 4

Ingredients:

- 2 large boiled potatoes
- 1/2 cup sour cream
- White pepper and salt to taste
- 1 cup cheddar cheese, shredded

Method:

1. Pierce the potatoes and add in sour cream.
2. Top with the cheese.
3. Drizzle pepper and salt.
4. Place them in a baking pan.
5. Bake at 82C or 180F for 5 minutes in the Cuisinart TOA-60 Convection Toaster Oven Airfryer.

Serving Suggestions: Serve by topping with pico de gallo.

Preparation & Cooking Tips: To have your baked potatoes in a firm shape, avoid peeling the potato skin.

4. Crispy Fillet

Preparation Time: 10 minutes

Cooking Time: 20 minutes

Servings: 4

Ingredients:
- 4 fish fillets
- 1 cup semolina
- 2 tbsp. vegetable oil
- ½ tbsp. paprika
- Pepper and salt to taste

Method:
1. Brush the fillets with oil.
2. Sprinkle paprika, pepper, and salt on both sides.
3. Dip each piece into the bowl of semolina.
4. Place them in a baking pan.
5. Choose the toaster setting in Cuisinart TOA-60 Convection Toaster Oven Airfryer.
6. Cook at 120C or 250F for 10 minutes.

Serving Suggestions: Squeeze a lemon and serve by adding some potato wedges on the side.

Preparation & Cooking Tips: For crunchier bites, toss in hot oil before serving.

5. Garlic Butter Baked Tilapia

Preparation Time: 10 minutes

Cooking Time: 15 minutes

Servings: 2

Ingredients:

- 2 tilapia fillets
- 1 tbsp. garlic paste
- 1 tbsp. onion paste
- 1 tbsp. parsley flakes
- ½ cup butter, melted
- Garlic pepper and salt to taste

Method:

1. Prepare a mixture of butter, parsley flakes, garlic, and onion paste.
2. Season the fillet with pepper and salt.
3. Array them in a baking pan.
4. Spout the prepared mixture onto them.
5. Set the broiler setting at 93C or 200F in the Cuisinart TOA-60 Convection Toaster Oven Airfryer.
6. Cook it for around 15 minutes.

Serving Suggestions: Serve with rice and stir-fried veggies.

Preparation & Cooking Tips: Add soy sauce to hit another level of deliciousness to the recipe.

6. Mediterranean Toasted Mushrooms

Preparation Time: 25 minutes

Cooking Time: 15 minutes

Servings: 6

Ingredients:
- 6 large mushrooms
- 2 tbsp. olive oil
- 1 egg
- 1 cup low-fat ricotta
- 3 shallots, diced
- 1 zucchini, grated
- 6 olives, chopped
- Few small tomatoes
- ½ cup basil, shredded
- 1 cup mozzarella cheese, grated
- Pepper and salt to taste

Method:
1. Cut the mushrooms in a flat shape.
2. Mix all the veggies with egg and season them well.
3. Settle the mixture gently in the mushroom roof.
4. Shred the cheese on top.
5. Add to the Cuisinart TOA-60 Convection Toaster Oven Airfryer.
6. Cook it for 15 minutes at 190C or 375F.

Serving Suggestions: Serve by drizzling some basil leaves on top.

Preparation & Cooking Tips: You can make it without cheese.

7. Creamy Pasta

Preparation Time: 15 minutes

Cooking Time: 35 minutes

Servings: 8

Ingredients:

- 4 cups uncooked pasta
- 4 cups marinara sauce
- 2 cups mozzarella cheese, shredded
- 1 cup Parmesan cheese, grated
- 1 cup ricotta cheese
- Salt to taste

Method:

1. Boil the pasta for 4/5 minutes, make sure to add salt.
2. Take a baking pan, pour a dollop of marinara sauce.
3. Add the boiled pasta into it, toss well to mix.
4. Shred the cheeses on top.
5. Choose the broiling setting in the Cuisinart TOA-60 Convection Toaster Oven Airfryer.
6. Bake at 180C or 350F for 35 minutes.

Serving Suggestions: Serve with mayonnaise and pico de gallo.

Preparation & Cooking Tips: Add chicken, shrimp, or veggies to enrich its flavor.

8. Broiled Momos

Preparation Time: 1 hour

Cooking Time: 35 minutes

Servings: 10

Ingredients:
- 4 cups flour
- 1 cup seawater
- 1½ cup chicken, smashed
- 2 cups cabbage, shredded
- 1 cup onion, chopped
- 1 tbsp. soya sauce

Method:
1. Combine the smashed chicken, cabbage and onion together.
2. Mix flour and salty water to make a dough.
3. Knead for at least 10 minutes.
4. Take a handful of dough and roll it into a round shape.
5. Spoon the filling in the middle of the shape.
6. Overlap the edges to cover the filling, pinch to seal.
7. Broil at 190C or 375F for 45 minutes in the Cuisinart TOA-60 Convection Toaster Oven Airfryer.

Serving Suggestions: Serve hot with salsa sauce.

Preparation & Cooking Tips: You can use lukewarm water and a pinch of salt instead of seawater.

9. Italian Cheesy Spaghetti Squash

Preparation Time: 20 minutes

Cooking Time: 50 minutes

Servings: 2

Ingredients:

- 1 spaghetti squash, divided
- 2 tbsp. olive oil
- 1½ cup Italian sausage
- 2 cups tomato sauce
- 1 cup mozzarella, shredded
- Pepper and salt to taste

Method:

1. Preheat the Cuisinart TOA-60 Convection Toaster Oven Airfryer to 190C or 375F.
2. Take one wall of spaghetti squash and scoop out the seeds.
3. Season it well and set to cook for around 30 minutes.
4. As it cools down, start shredding to pierce the center.
5. Fill the hovels with tomato sauce and Italian sausage.
6. Top with cheese and leave it to cook for another 10 minutes.

Serving Suggestions: Serve with spreading some Bombay mix on top.

Preparation & Cooking Tips: Add 1 tbsp. of liquid smoke to fetch a smoky grilled flavor to the recipe.

10. Pepperoni Delight Pizza

Preparation Time: 25 minutes
Cooking Time: 40 minutes
Servings: 4
Ingredients:

- 2 ½ cups flour
- 2 tbsp. olive oil
- 1 tbsp. activate dry yeast
- 1 cup lukewarm water
- 1 tbsp. sugar
- 2 cups tomato sauce
- 1 cup pepperoni
- 1 cups mozzarella cheese, shredded
- Pepper and salt to taste

Method:

1. Preheat the Cuisinart TOA-60 Convection Toaster Oven Airfryer to 250C or 420F.
2. Mix sugar in the warm water, dissolve the yeast into it.
3. Let it stand for 10 minutes or until it becomes frothy.
4. Now add it into the mixture of flour, oil and salt.
5. Knead for 5 minutes and leave it to ferment.
6. Roll it to a round shape.
7. Spread the sauce.
8. Add the toppings.
9. Bake for 40 minutes.

Serving Suggestions: Serve with ketchups and mayonnaise on the side.

Preparation & Cooking Tips: When you set the dough for fermentation, make sure to use a plastic wrap to cover the dough.

Chapter 7: Roasting Recipes

1. Roasted Chipotle-Lime Shrimp

Preparation Time: 10 minutes

Cooking Time: 45 minutes

Servings: 5

Ingredients:
- 1 lb. shrimp
- ½ lb. potato
- ½ lb. broccolini
- ½ lb. asparagus
- 3 limes
- 1 teaspoon chipotle pepper seasoning
- 3 tablespoon butter

Method:
1. Choose the bake setting and set the Cuisinart TOA-60 Convection Toaster Oven Airfryer to 180C or 350F.
2. Meanwhile, chop up the veggies.
3. Thoroughly season the veggies and shrimp with chipotle pepper, and place it on a greased tray.
4. Roast for about 45 minutes.

Serving Suggestion: Serve piping hot with some fresh cilantro on top.

Preparation and Cooking Tips: Don't throw out the roasted limes and squeeze them over the dish for an added zing of flavor.

2. Deviled Chicken

Preparation Time: 10 minutes

Cooking Time: 50 minutes

Serving: 5

Ingredients:
- 6 chicken legs
- 1/4 cup melted butter
- 1 tablespoon ground mustard
- 1 teaspoon paprika
- Salt and pepper to taste

Method:
1. Choose the broil setting and preheat the Cuisinart TOA-60 Convection Toaster Oven Airfryer to 200C or 400F.
2. Place the chicken legs into a big pan.
3. In a bowl, combine all the remaining ingredients and pour it over the chicken.
4. Cook for 50 minutes, flipping occasionally.

Serving Suggestion: Serve with some veggies on the side.

Preparation and Cooking Tips: Baste the chicken constantly with pan juices for a more flavorful outcome.

3. Cheddar Bacon Chicken

Preparation Time: 5 minutes

Cooking Time: 10 minutes

Serving: 5

Ingredients:
- 5 boneless chicken breasts
- 1/2 cup teriyaki sauce
- 1/2 cup barbecue sauce
- 5 slices bacon
- 5 slices cheddar cheese

Method:
1. Choose the broil setting in the Cuisinart TOA-60 Convection Toaster Oven Airfryer and preheat to 230C or 450F.
2. Combine the teriyaki and barbecue sauce and dip the chicken in it.
3. Top one slice of bacon and cheese on top of each chicken piece.
4. Roast for 10 minutes.

Serving Suggestion: Spread some more barbecue sauce over chicken before serving.

Preparation and Cooking Tips: Use sharp cheddar cheese for more flavor.

4. Herb-Roasted Turkey

Preparation Time: 10 minutes

Cooking Time: 60 minutes

Serving: 5

Ingredients:

- 1 lb. turkey breast
- 2 tablespoons soy sauce
- 1 teaspoon pepper
- 3 tablespoon Italian herb seasoning
- 1/2 cup butter
- Salt to taste

Method:

1. Choose the bake setting and set the Cuisinart TOA-60 Convection Toaster Oven Airfryer to 150C or 300F.
2. Place the turkey in a roasting pan.
3. Combine all the sauce, butter, and spices.
4. Drizzle the turkey with butter mixture.
5. Roast for 1 hour.

Serving Suggestion: Serve with gravy or any sauce of your choice.

Preparation and Cooking Tips: Let the turkey stand for 15 minutes before carving.

5. Roasted Whole Chicken

Preparation Time: 10 minutes

Cooking Time: 60 minutes

Serving: 6

Ingredients:

- 2.5 lb. whole chicken
- 1/2 teaspoon pepper
- 1/2 teaspoon onion salt
- 1/2 teaspoon celery salt
- 1/2 teaspoon seasoned salt

Method:

1. Preheat the Cuisinart TOA-60 Convection Toaster Oven Airfryer to 230C or 450F.
2. Mix the seasonings and rub it all over the chicken.
3. Tie the drumsticks with a length of twine.
4. Roast for about an hour.

Serving Suggestion: Serve with some creamy mashed potatoes on the side.

Preparation and Cooking Tips: If the chicken starts to brown too quickly, cover it with aluminium foil.

6. Roasted Herb Salmon

Preparation Time: 5 minutes

Cooking Time: 15 minutes

Serving: 6

Ingredients:

- 1 lb. salmon fillet
- 3 tablespoon butter
- 3 cloves of garlic, minced
- 1 tablespoon rosemary leaves
- 1 tablespoon thyme leaves
- Salt and pepper to taste

Method:

1. Choose the broil setting and set the Cuisinart TOA-60 Convection Toaster Oven Airfryer to 180C or 350F.
2. Place the salmon in a large pan.
3. Combine all the remaining ingredients and brush it over the salmon.
4. Cook for about 15 minutes.

Serving Suggestion: Sprinkle some freshly chopped parsley on top and serve immediately.

Preparation and Cooking Tips: Wrap the fillet with foil to prevent any sticking and burning.

7. Roasted Chicken and Stuffing

Preparation Time: 5 minutes

Cooking Time: 50 minutes

Serving: 6

Ingredients:

- 6 chicken thighs
- 1 lb. potatoes, cubed
- 1/2 lb. brussels sprout
- 1 lb. carrot, cubed
- 3 tablespoon Italian herbs
- 1 tablespoon onion salt
- 3 tablespoon olive oil

Method:

1. Set the Cuisinart TOA-60 Convection Toaster Oven Airfryer to its airfry function and preheat to 230C or 450F.
2. Place the veggies and chicken in a baking dish.
3. Season well with salt, herbs, and oil.
4. Cook for 40 minutes, flipping the chicken occasionally.

Serving Suggestion: Serve hot with a side of some wild rice.

Preparation and Cooking Tips: Make sure to not overcook the chicken if you don't want the meat to be chewy.

8. Roasted stone fruits

Preparation Time: 5 minutes

Cooking Time: 30 minutes

Serving: 5

Ingredients:

- 1 lb. stone fruits, chopped
- ½ cup brown sugar
- 3 tablespoon maple syrup

Method:

1. Choose the bake setting and preheat the Cuisinart TOA-60 Convection Toaster Oven Airfryer to 180C or 350F.
2. Place the fruits in a tray and toss it with sugar and maple syrup.
3. Roast for 30 minutes.

Serving Suggestion: Add a dollop of ice cream on top while serving.

Preparation and Cooking Tips: Freeze the fruits for a while before serving.

9. Roasted Ham and Veggies

Preparation Time: 5 minutes

Cooking Time: 30 minutes

Serving: 6

Ingredients:
- 6 slices hams
- 6 potatoes, cubed
- 6 carrots, cubed
- 1 large onion, diced
- Salt and pepper to taste
- 1 tablespoon olive oil

Method:
1. Set the Cuisinart TOA-60 Convection Toaster Oven Airfryer to its broil setting and preheat to 180C or 350F.
2. In a large baking tray, combine all the ingredients together.
3. Cook for 30 minutes.

Serving Suggestion: Sprinkle some more pepper on top and serve immediately.

Preparation and Cooking Tips: You can use sweet potatoes in this recipe as a substitute for the potatoes.

10. Roasted Chicken Fajitas

Preparation Time: 5 minutes

Cooking Time: 15 minutes

Serving: 5

Ingredients:
- 3 lb. boneless chicken breast, cubed
- 1 large onion, diced
- 3 cup bell pepper, julienned
- 1 teaspoon ground cumin
- 1/2 teaspoon oregano
- 1 tablespoon soy sauce
- 1 tablespoon Worcestershire sauce

Method:
1. Choose the broil setting and preheat the Cuisinart TOA-60 Convection Toaster Oven Airfryer to 180C or 350F.
2. In a greased baking tray, place the chicken and veggies.
3. In a small bowl, combine the remaining ingredients.
4. Pour the mixture on the tray.
5. Cook for 15 minutes, stirring occasionally.

Serving Suggestion: Serve hot with some sour cream on top.

Preparation and Cooking Tips: To up the spice level of this dish, add some taco seasoning to the recipe.

Chapter 8: Desserts and Snacks

1. S'mores Bars

Preparation Time: 15 minutes

Cooking Time: 20 minutes

Servings: 12

Ingredients:

- ½ cup butter
- 2 cups graham crackers, crushed
- 1 cup milk chocolate chips
- 1 tbsp. vanilla extract
- 1/3 cup sugar
- 1 cup marshmallows

Method:

1. Beat the butter and sugar until the mixture gets fluffy.
2. Add in the vanilla extract and ½ cup graham cracks, mix.
3. Spread the remaining crushed crackers in a baking pan, lay out the marshmallows.
4. Pour the made mixture and sprinkle over the chocolate chips.
5. Use bake setting in the Cuisinart TOA-60 Convection Toaster Oven Airfryer at 180C or 350F for 20 minutes.

Serving Suggestions: Serve with chocolate frosting on top.

Preparation & Cooking Tips: Add 1-3 tbsp. of condensed milk to make it sweeter.

2. Red Velvet Cheesecake

Preparation Time: 35 minutes

Cooking Time: 1 hour

Servings: 8

Ingredients:
- 1 packet Oreo, crushed
- ½ cup butter
- 1 egg
- ½ cup buttermilk
- 1 cup sour cream
- 2 cups sugar
- 3 tbsp. cocoa powder
- 2 tbsp. vanilla extract
- 1-ounce food color, red

Method:
1. Wrap a baking pan with foil.
2. Layer oreo crumbs.
3. Beat the rest ingredients together to a smooth batter and pour onto the prepared pan.
4. Take a larger baking pan and add 1 inch of hot water into that to make a water bath.
5. Use bake of the Cuisinart TOA-60 Convection Toaster Oven Airfryer at 160C or 325F for 1 hour.

Serving Suggestions: Serve with buttercream.

Preparation & Cooking Tips: Refrigerate the batter overnight.

3. Broiled Custards

Preparation Time: 20 minutes

Cooking Time: 10 minutes

Servings: 4

Ingredients:
- 2 large eggs
- 3 cups sugar
- 1½ cups whipping cream

Method:
1. Drizzle ½ cup sugar in a broiling pan evenly.
2. Caramelize the sugar with a torch.
3. Beat the rest of the sugar, eggs, and cream for 10 minutes.
4. Pour the batter into the caramelized pan.
5. Choose the broiler setting in the Cuisinart TOA-60 Convection Toaster Oven Airfryer.
6. Set it to 160C or 325F for 10 minutes.

Serving Suggestions: Serve with strawberries and toast on the side.

Preparation & Cooking Tips: Use 1 tbsp. vanilla extract to remove the eggy smell

4. Jelly Kolachkes

Preparation Time: 1 hour

Cooking Time: 15 minutes

Servings: 10

Ingredients:
- 1 cup butter
- Colorful jellies
- 3 cups flour
- 2 tbsp. sugar

Method:
1. Mix flour, butter, sugar, and salt to make a dough.
2. Roll the dough into a 12x10 inch rectangle shape.
3. Cut into 2-inch squares and fill the center with jelly.
4. Overlap two reverse corners and seal.
5. Arrange them in a baking pan.
6. Use bake of the Cuisinart TOA-60 Convection Toaster Oven Airfryer at 180C or 350F for 15 minutes.

Serving Suggestions: Serve with white chocolate dipping.

Preparation & Cooking Tips: Experiment with the fillings! Try hazelnut spread!

5. Cassava Cake

Preparation Time: 8 minutes

Cooking Time: 1 hour 10 minutes

Servings: 8

Ingredients:
- 2 cups cassava, thawed
- 1½ cup coconut, desiccated
- 1 can condensed milk
- 1 can vaporized milk
- 1 can coconut milk
- 1 cup sugar
- 1 egg

Method:
1. Preheat the Cuisinart TOA-60 Convection Toaster Oven Airfryer to 190C or 375F.
2. Combine all the ingredients and beat well.
3. Pour the batter into a well-greased baking pan.
4. Use bake setting for 1 hour 10 minutes.

Serving Suggestions: Serve with chocolate syrup on top.

Preparation & Cooking Tips: Add a pinch of cumin powder to add a tempting aroma.

6. Choco Lava Cake

Preparation Time: 20 minutes

Cooking Time: 12 minutes

Servings: 4

Ingredients:
- 2½ cup butter, cubed
- ½ cup chocolate, crushed
- 2 cups flour
- 2 cups sugar
- 1 egg

Method:
1. Preheat the Cuisinart TOA-60 Convection Toaster Oven Airfryer to 230C or 450F.
2. Melt the chocolate and ½ cup butter, and mix together.
3. Beat the butter with egg, sugar, and flour together.
4. Add in the choco butter mixture.
5. Pour the batter into ramekins.
6. Use bake setting for 12 minutes.

Serving Suggestions: Serve with icing sugar on top.

Preparation & Cooking Tips: Refrigerate the batter for a few hours before mixing the choco butter mixture.

7. Sticky Peanut Bars

Preparation Time: 20 minutes

Cooking Time: 30 minutes

Servings: 15

Ingredients:

- 1 cup butter
- 2 cups baking flour
- 1 cup packed brown sugar
- 2 cups salted peanuts
- 1 cup chocolate chips

Method:

1. Preheat the Cuisinart TOA-60 Convection Toaster Oven Airfryer to 180C or 350F.
2. Beat the butter and sugar in a bowl.
3. Add baking flour into it, and mix well.
4. Pour the batter into a baking pan and leave it to bake for 20 minutes.
5. Arrange the peanuts and choco chips on top and bake for another 10 minutes.

Serving Suggestions: Serve with chocolate syrup on top.

Preparation & Cooking Tips: To make it crunchier, add ½ tbsp. of baking soda in the batter.

8. Lemon-Lime Bars

Preparation Time: 20 minutes

Cooking Time: 15 minutes

Servings: 8

Ingredients:

- 1 cup butter
- 2 tbsp. lime zest, grated
- 1 cup lemon juice
- 2 cups flour
- 2 egg
- 3 cups sugar

Method:

1. Preheat the Cuisinart TOA-60 Convection Toaster Oven Airfryer to 180C or 350F.
2. Mix all ingredients.
3. Take a ramekin, fill ¼ of it and set to bake.
4. Add the lemon juice.
5. When the bars seem lightly browned pour more batter into it.
6. Use bake for 20-25 minutes.

Serving Suggestions: Serve with sprinkling lemon zest and icing on top.

Preparation & Cooking Tips: If you don't want a crunchy crust, bake this dessert only once.

9. Pumpkin Roll

Preparation Time: 15 minutes

Cooking Time: 20 minutes

Servings: 15

Ingredients:
- 1 cup butter
- 2 cups canned pumpkin
- 1½ cup sugar
- 2 egg
- 2 cups flour
- 1 tbsp. baking powder
- 1 cup pecans, chopped

Method:
1. Choose the broiler setting in Cuisinart TOA-60 Convection Toaster Oven Airfryer and preheat to 180C or 350F.
2. Beat all the ingredients except the pecans.
3. Spread the batter into a pan.
4. Add the pecans.
5. Bake for 20 minutes.
6. Place the cake into a towel and roll up the cake.
7. Refrigerate for an hour.

Serving Suggestions: Re-roll the cake and serve by cutting it into slices.

Preparation & Cooking Tips: Sieve the pumpkin puree for smoothness.

10. Cherry Crumble

Preparation Time: 15 minutes

Cooking Time: 20 minutes

Servings: 5

Ingredients:
- 3 cups cherries
- ⅓ cup butter
- ½ cup sugar
- 1 cup baking flour
- 1 tbsp. ground nutmeg
- 1 tbsp. ground cinnamon

Method:
1. Preheat the Cuisinart TOA-60 Convection Toaster Oven Airfryer to 180C or 350F.
2. Mix cherries and sugar.
3. Mix the flour and butter.
4. Place the cherry mixture in a baking pan.
5. Pour the flour mixture on top.
6. Sprinkle nutmeg and cinnamon.
7. Bake for 20 minutes.

Serving Suggestions: Serve with a scoop of ice cream on the side.

Preparation & Cooking Tips: Lemon juice will add a tangy kick.

Conclusion

We are sure that by now you have a clear understanding and idea about all the incredible recipes that you can try with the Cuisinart TOA-60 Convection Toaster Oven Airfryer.

On top of that, we have also mentioned everything that you possibly need to know about operating the equipment anyway, so we doubt that you will have any other issue in regard to the product's operation and functions.

But anyway, before attempting to cook anything in the tCuisinart TOA-60 Convection Toaster Oven Airfryer, make sure to follow all the tips and tricks that we mentioned previously in this cookbook so that you do not come across any technical malfunction while cooking up something awesome and delicious!

So, what are you waiting for? Get on your heels and get whatever ingredient you need to cook something incredible with the help of this cookbook today!

CPSIA information can be obtained
at www.ICGtesting.com
Printed in the USA
LVHW061032140122
708080LV00011B/92